4A76

PHILIP LARKIN

PHILIP LARKIN

by

ALAN BROWNJOHN

Edited by Ian Scott-Kilvert

PUBLISHED FOR
THE BRITISH COUNCIL
BY LONGMAN GROUP LTD

LONGMAN GROUP LTD
Longman House, Burnt Mill, Harlow, Essex

*Associated companies, branches and
representatives throughout the world*

First published 1975
© Alan Brownjohn 1975

*Printed in England by
Bradleys, Reading and London*

ISBN 0 582 01247 3

PHILIP LARKIN

I

IN HIS very funny and self-revealing poem 'I Remember, I Remember', from *The Less Deceived*, Philip Larkin dashes any supposition that he may have had an eventful, or romantic, or conventionally poetic early life. Sardonically, he denies, in turn, any childhood visionary experiences, any release into entertaining adventure from the routines of family living, any overwhelming first-love recollections—

> The bracken where I never trembling sat,
>
> Determined to go through with it; where she
> Lay back, and 'all became a burning mist'.

—any hint whatsoever of juvenile genius detected and nurtured by discerning elders. Larkin's down-to-earth contention is that his formative years were monumentally ordinary. There were so few excitements that he can, he feels, truthfully describe his childhood as 'unspent'; meaning that it scarcely happened at all.

The poem is partly a rejoinder to all those fanciful, autobiographical excursions in which writers have traced in their childhood all the magical stirrings of their later talent. But it is also, underneath the humour, a considered personal statement about how Larkin sees both life and poetry. It has never been a matter of blinding revelations, mystical insights, expectations glitteringly fulfilled. Life, for Larkin and, implicitly, for all of us, is something lived mundanely, with a gradually accumulating certainty that its golden prizes are sheer illusion, that second best things will have to suffice.

As a poet he has taken as his themes such things as the gap between human hope and cold reality; the illusory nature of choice in life; frustration with one's lot in a present which is dismal, and in face of a future which brings only age and death. Against all this, on the positive side, he can only set images of a personal, or a national, past in which life was

3

more ordered and attractive than it is now; a reverence for places and activities which contain and perpetuate the deepest and best human feelings; and certain indefinable images of purity and serenity, known mostly at solitary moments, which enable him to rise above the soiled terrain of living. It may seem unlikely ground on which to build major poetry. But Larkin has produced the most technically brilliant and resonantly beautiful, profoundly disturbing yet appealing and approachable, body of verse of any English poet in the last twenty-five years.

Larkin's 'unspent' childhood was lived in Coventry, where he was born in 1922 to parents in the professional middle class (his father was the City Treasurer). It would indeed seem, if one puts together the details from the one or two autobiographical pieces he has published, that Larkin's early years, like most people's, were typical rather than remarkable. There were no indications of the child prodigy, but plenty of the expected boyhood enthusiasms (playing with model trains, collecting cigarette cards, following cricket fanatically). One early ambition was to be a jazz drummer. He was educated in a very good, staid grammar school which uncovered no literary flair, though he contributed humorous prose monologues and poems to the magazine. Larkin writes of reading at this period 'at the rate of a book a day, even despite the tiresome interruptions of morning and afternoon school'. Eventually he deserted his drumming ambitions

. . . to settle upon a literary career . . . I wrote ceaselessly . . . now verse, which I sewed up into little books, now prose, a thousand words a night after homework, resting my foolscap on Beethoven's Op. 132, the only classical album I possessed.

From school he went up to read English at St John's College, Oxford, in 1940, a wartime undergraduate of eighteen who expected to be called into the armed forces before long. Larkin recalls the atmosphere of austerity, and the unsophisticated boyishness of his undergraduate generation. But in terms of friendship and stimulation from his student peers, this wartime university education seems to have denied him little. Among his friends were the novelist

4

Kingsley Amis, the science-fiction writer Edmund Crispin (Bruce Montgomery), the poet Alan Ross, the politician Edward du Cann. Failing his army medical, he was able to complete his Oxford years without interruption, and took first-class honours in 1943.

Larkin's subsequent career has been as outwardly un-eventful as his early life: librarian's posts in a public library in Wellington, Shropshire, and then in academic libraries at the University of Leicester (then the University College) and Queen's University, Belfast. He became the Librarian in the Brynmor Jones Library of the University of Hull in 1955, a post which he still occupies. Deliberately, but fully in keeping with his temperament and inclination, Larkin has resisted that element of public living which opens itself as an opportunity or a snare for many poets, as their talent and fame develops. He has avoided the poetry-reading circuits completely (declaring shyly but emphatically, in 1973, when persuaded to read his celebrated poem 'The Whitsun Weddings' before a studio audience for a radio broadcast, that 'this is the first time I've ever read a poem in public and if I have any say in the matter it'll be the last'.

He has written little about his own verse, though he prefaces his readings on the record made of the complete book *The Whitsun Weddings* with some fascinating comment, and some of his jazz reviews and occasional literary criticism throw light on both the writings and the personality. Awards (including the Queen's Gold Medal for Poetry) and critical esteem have come to this very private man without his striving after them, leaving him modestly surprised that such things should have come to him at all.

II

The poems in Larkin's first volume, *The North Ship* (1945), are indisputably those of a private, solitary person. Though full of interest, *The North Ship* is not a very good book, and comparison with the vigorous scene-setting and character-ization of Larkin's first novel, *Jill*, published one year later, would have suggested at the time that his talent lay in fiction rather than poetry. At the same time, critical attempts to separate it entirely from the later Larkin, as something quite untypical as well as inferior, are mistaken.

Introducing the new edition of 1966 (with slyly amusing reference to the circumstances of its original publication), Larkin sees in the poems evidence of 'not one abandoned self but several'—the ex-schoolboy for whom Auden was the modern master, the undergraduate looking to Dylan Thomas, and 'the immediately post-Oxford self, isolated in Shropshire with a complete Yeats stolen from the local girls' school'. But though there are certainly signs of all these poets (the first and third in style and content, the second in the realm of nature which the poems mostly inhabit), there is never any slavish imitation, conscious or unconscious. And already the voice has some characteristic Larkin tones which will be heard again in each of his later, mature volumes; especially at those crucial moments of removal from the real world into a purer because more lonely existence.

The North Ship has thirty-one poems. Of these twenty-three are simply and self-effacingly numbered and of the remainder some have non-committal titles such as 'Dawn', 'Winter' and 'Night Music'—never a good tactic for leaving a clear impression on the reader's mind. In fact, the impression left by *The North Ship* is that of a poet struggling sensitively—with unambitious technical care rather than verbal energy or imaginative stamina—to pit some private experiences of exhilaration and release, or some recurrent images of purity and vitality in nature, against the dullness of ordinary, solitary existence and the prevailing sense of death; so the later Larkin *is* here, though writ very small. Poem I celebrates spring and renewal only to curtail its strenuous bursts of joy with a mildly forbidding Yeatsian refrain:

> Every one thing,
> Shape, colour and voice,
> Cries out, Rejoice!
>   *A drum taps: a wintry drum.*

The earth, in III, contains nothing as pure as the simple light of the full moon, an idea to which Larkin will return

6

much later; and the same earth is most 'brilliant' (VII) when it is most 'unearthly'. In IX, a sonnet, Larkin submits himself exultantly to the music of nature, the wind and air in a high place, as a Romantic poet might; but is carried back relentlessly to the harder human world:

> How to recall such music, when the street
> Darkens? Among the rain and stone places
> I find only an ancient sadness falling,
> Only hurrying and troubled faces,
> The walking of girls' vulnerable feet,
> The heart in its own endless silence kneeling.

The enjoyment of being solitary, the sad faces of the urban crowd, the abjectness of the heart expressed in the effective final line recur frequently in *The North Ship*, and will all crop up again in the later Larkin, though not quite in the same form. The 'Ugly Sister' of poem XIX (who is 'not bewitched in adolescence/And brought to love') will, for example, return as the isolated figure in the later books who is constantly preferring the silences of nature to the conversation of people, his own company to that of others. The parting lovers of X, XXIV, XXV and XXX will again be separated, by time, space and the protagonist's sense of his own inability to love, in several more arresting poems in subsequent volumes.

There are other elements of continuity from the vein of *The North Ship* which are worth noting. The remarkable —remarkably optimistic—'Wedding Wind' in *The Less Deceived* reads like a full-bodied version of one of the brief, cryptic 'situation' poems in the first book. And clear parallels in the nature of the imagery and its uses can be made with poems like 'Dry Point' (sexual imagery opposed to a metaphor of light representing purity and freedom) and 'Absences' (sea imagery providing a link between the strained celebration of natural forces in *The North Ship* and some powerful, intensely mysterious features of a poem like 'Livings' (II) in *High Windows*).

But what will not be repeated is the clear debt to Auden in the untypical allegory employed in 'Conscript' (X), or the Yeats-like cadences of XIII and XX. Larkin ascribes the weaknesses of *The North Ship* to the power of Yeats's influence ('pervasive as garlic') and any improvement at that time to his new-found admiration for the poetry of Thomas Hardy. But 'Waiting for Breakfast', a further poem added at the end of the new edition of *The North Ship* (written a year after the others and showing 'the Celtic fever abated and the patient sleeping soundly') is a fully-developed achievement of the mature Larkin, who is a very individual poet indeed. And the main difference between *The North Ship* and the books which follow it (three only, so far, brought out at ten-year intervals) is that the first volume, despite flashes of promise, contains scarcely anything that is more than fragmentary and tentative. The poems are mostly short, the full, authentic Larkin voice is only heard faintly (if still more distinctly than anyone else's) and the later themes are only hinted at. The abundant technical expertise has not yet come into operation. Above all, the typical Larkin, protagonist—humorous, self-deprecatory, observant—seems shyly reluctant to show himself.

After *The North Ship* Larkin endeavoured unsuccessfully, for a few years, to publish a second book of poems with the title *In the Grip of Light*. Finally, he sent out in 1951 a privately issued pamphlet, *XX Poems*, which attracted no public attention at all, even though several poems in it were later to be praised in his hardback volume, *The Less Deceived*. This book, a collection of twenty-nine poems, was venturesomely published by the little Marvell Press in Hull in 1955, when the poet was thirty-two, and the change and improvement since the early book is instantly apparent. One gains an immediate sense, from the first page, of growing technical command and range (in the highly-wrought nine-line stanza of 'Church Going' and the witty, terse quatrains of 'Toads'); of greater substance, and of a careful, sensitive thoroughness in the working through of ideas (in work as different as the reflective, nostalgic love poem 'Maiden Name' and 'Poetry of Departures', with its mordant observations on freedom of action). There is now, for the first time, a thread of wry, decidedly disconcerting humour ('I Remember, I Remember'; and 'If, my Darling', where he writes at once nakedly and bizarrely about private quirks and fears). There is some lovingly detailed observation of a real world ('At Grass' and 'Church Going' again). But the largest difference is summed up in a new ability to convince and to move the reader through the confidence of a fully-developed poetic personality; because Larkin has now discovered that it is perfectly valid, and indeed liberating, to be entirely himself, using his own language.

The poem of which the closing lines provide the title of the book is called 'Deceptions'. It is concerned with the drugging and rape of a young girl in the London of the last century: Henry Mayhew's *London Labour and the London Poor* provides the epigraph. This choice of a very specific starting-point, together with the direct manner of the poet's compassionate address to the girl, immediately distinguishes the poem from any in *The North Ship*:

> Even so distant, I can taste the grief,
> Bitter and sharp with stalks, he made you gulp.
> The sun's occasional print, the brisk brief
> Worry of wheels along the street outside
> Where bridal London bows the other way,
> And light, unanswerable and tall and wide,
> Forbids the scar to heal . . .

The unobtrusively adept play of rhyme and rhythm, the studied appropriateness of diction and imagery (the exact pathos of 'Where bridal London bows the other way' and the characteristic Larkin light image) are the hallmarks of the poet's mature style. And the message the poem proceeds to offer is also characteristic:

> What can be said,
> Except that suffering is exact, but where
> Desire takes charge, readings will grow erratic?
> For you would hardly care
> That you were less deceived, out on that bed,
> Than he was, stumbling up the breathless stair
> To burst into fulfilment's desolate attic.

Consolatory comment would be irrelevant, but one can at least be certain that the rapist would have known desolation more bitter after the fulfilment of his desires.

In varying forms, the idea here is a recurrent and important one in Larkin. The recognized rewards and goals in life are deceptions. This applies not only to crude sexual success or worldly fame, but acknowledged ends such as happiness in marriage, or among social groups. It is more sensible not to strive for such things. In *The Less Deceived*, 'Places, Loved Ones' advises against hoping for the ideal circumstances of life to arrive:

> wiser to keep away
> From thinking you still might trace
> Uncalled-for to this day
> Your person, your place.

'Wires' tells of the young, and hopeful cattle (but it is not only cattle) who, 'scenting purer water', blunder up against electric fences which turn them into old cattle from that moment. And the marvellous and haunting 'Next, Please' (the first of numerous ironically sinister Larkin titles) argues that life's 'sparkling armada of promises' is an illusion in face of death:

> Only one ship is seeking us, a black-
> Sailed unfamiliar, towing at her back
> A huge and birdless silence. In her wake
> No waters breed or break.

There will often, however, be some degree of self-reproach and self-questioning at not somehow having managed to contrive a different kind of existence from the sober one he finds himself landed with. Being average, ordinary, even dull may be just what you would wish for a child (in 'Born Yesterday'), if that brings more happiness than the possession of high talents or other 'uncustomary' qualities. But Larkin acutely senses, at this stage in his writing, a dilemma of choice between a life of risk and adventure and the steady rituals of secure employment. In two entertaining and challenging pieces, 'Toads' and 'Poetry of Departures', he examines the possibility of getting away from the plodding, timid world of work and home:

Why should I let the toad *work*
    Squat on my life?
Can't I use my wit as a pitchfork
    And drive the brute off?

Six days of the week it soils
    With its sickening poison—
Just for paying a few bills!
    That's out of proportion.

('Toads')

*   *   *

We all hate home
And having to be there:
I detest my room,
Its specially-chosen junk,
The good books, the good bed,
And my life, in perfect order:
So to hear it said

He walked out on the whole crowd
Leaves me flushed and stirred,
Like *Then she undid her dress*
Or *Take that you bastard*;
Surely I can, if he did?

('Poetry of Departures')

Larkin's vigorous colloquial mode here, blended subtly
with serious, nicely-paced argument, catches the momentary
intensity of people's frustration with their routines. But in
the end, in both poems, the speaker decides he cannot make
the break. Something toad-like inside him prevents it, or
else he analyses (rationalizes?) this desire to get away from it
all as 'artificial'. Nevertheless, the dilemma does not go away,
and is closely bound up with the virtual impossibility of
sorting out matters like time, freedom of will, the seizing of
life's opportunities. In 'Triple Time', the present moment,
soured and uneventful as it is, was what one looked forward
to in childhood as a time of 'adult enterprise'; but in the
future it will come to resemble

A valley cropped by fat neglected chances
That we insensately forbore to fleece.

11

All these are common attitudes, dilemmas and con-
clusions, and much of the appeal of *The Less Deceived* lay in
Larkin's ability to define them and enclose them in a poetry
very much that of 'a man speaking to men'. The larger the
questions about the nature and purpose of human existence
become, the more impressive the poem: he rises more
impressively to the large themes with each succeeding
volume. The most important poem in *The Less Deceived* is
certainly 'Church Going', about visiting a church in an age
when religion no longer seems valid. The separation of the
words in the title is deliberate, since the poet, having stepped
awkwardly into the building, looked vaguely around it
and donated (it is legal tender, but faintly disrespectful in
what is probably an Ulster Protestant church), 'an Irish
sixpence', starts wondering

> When churches fall completely out of use
> What we shall turn them into, if we shall keep
> A few cathedrals chronically on show,
> Their parchment, plate and pyx in locked cases,
> And let the rest rent-free to rain and sheep.
> Shall we avoid them as unlucky places?

The poem moves through this from its deceptively casual
and distantly ironical opening to a grave and beautiful
conclusion. The church deserves reverence as a kind of
repository of the profoundest human feelings, which *should*
somehow be invested in one spot:

> it held unspilt
> So long and equably what since is found
> Only in separation—marriage, and birth,
> And death, and thoughts of these

It therefore has the feel of a symbol of an ordered and
stable society (Larkin's small 'c' conservatism here makes
its first showing in his verse); something lost in our own less
innocent, more brash, more disorganized times.

> A serious house on serious earth it is,
> In whose blent air all our compulsions meet,
> Are recognized, and robed as destinies.

And that much never can be obsolete,
Since someone will forever be surprising
A hunger in himself to be more serious,
And gravitating with it to this ground,
Which, he once heard, was proper to grow wise in,
If only that so many dead lie round.

Much of Larkin's best poetry in his next two books caters for
that 'hunger to be serious'.

III

The reputation Larkin established with *The Less Deceived*
was triumphantly confirmed by his next volume of poems.
Although he has eschewed the idea of 'development' as a
necessity for a poet, *The Whitsun Weddings* (1964) con-
spicuously carries his own progress several stages further.
The technical range and finesse is ever more apparent. The
blend of instantly recognizable social reality and a strongly
individual slant on life is given us in a collection of poems
which are the most accessible Larkin had so far produced;
however, the full implications of a Larkin poem rarely yield
themselves up at first reading, and there have been some
notable misunderstandings of his intention where he has
adopted a *persona*.

The captivating accuracy with which he catches the
physical feel of life in England in our time in *The Whitsun
Weddings* (look at poems like 'Here', or 'The Large Cool
Store', or 'Essential Beauty') led to considerable praise for
Larkin as a social observer. This was entirely merited. It
also led to the bestowal of the label 'social poet'. This was
unhelpful, since it suggested concerns Larkin did not have,
and boundaries to poetry which was all the time expanding
in scope.

In each of his three mature collections of verse Larkin has
given us one longer poem which lays claim to major status.
If in *The Less Deceived* it was 'Church Going' (and later, in
High Windows, it is to be 'The Building') the title-poem itself
occupies that place in *The Whitsun Weddings*. The social
detail, the whole sense of people and landscape, is rendered

infallibly. Yet this sort of observation is far from being the whole point of the poem. Larkin's own position is that of a different kind of observer, one standing a little distance away from the happiness of others, unable to feel affinity with them, yet cautiously assuming such joy as they may be able to find. Such a stance is one of the 'positives' in Larkin's poetry, which we may balance against the powerful articulations of despair.

The other people here are newly-married couples, joining the poet's train on the journey to London one hot Whit Saturday, and drawn to his attention by the noise of rowdy send-offs on station platforms:

> The fathers with broad belts under their suits
> And seamy foreheads; mothers loud and fat;
> An uncle shouting smut; and then the perms,
> The nylon gloves and jewellery-substitutes,
> The lemons, mauves and olive-ochres that
>
> Marked off the girls unreally from the rest.

Larkin sees it detachedly: first with amusement (though without superiority or priggishness), then with wryly penetrating comment on what the moment means to each participant ('children frowned/At something dull; fathers had never known/Success so huge and wholly farcical'). And lastly, as the train approaches London, he draws the poem to a climax with these solemnly beautiful thoughts on the married futures of the dozen or so couples travelling with him:

> it was nearly done, this frail
> Travelling coincidence; and what it held
> Stood ready to be loosed with all the power
> That being changed can give. We slowed again,
> And as the tightened brakes took hold, there swelled
> A sense of falling, like an arrow-shower
> Sent out of sight, somewhere becoming rain.

As in 'Church Going' he has moved from the position of the slightly ironical witness to that of the thoroughly involved thinker, searching out the deeper meaning of what he has seen. And though that 'sense of falling' is ambiguous (falling *is* an uncomfortable thing), the suggestion of the change wrought in human destinies by carrying through certain observances, the hint of fruition achieved *somewhere* (that 'arrow-shower/Sent out of sight, somewhere becoming rain') pays the same sort of tentative, yet real, tribute to the validity of some human rituals. We shall see more of this.

For all that, and despite the kind of hesitant affirmation he makes at the end of a lovely and remarkable poem like 'An Arundel Tomb', the prevailing air of *The Whitsun Weddings* as a collection is bleak. The good things (the innocence before the cataclysm of 'MCMXIV', New Orleans jazz in 'For Sidney Bechet') are almost always of the past, to be regarded with resigned nostalgia. The realities of the present are mainly dispiriting, and human hope is drained away by time. But hope does still exist, in one important sense, in Larkin: in the humane precision with which hope*less* things are observed. A poem like 'Faith Healing' concentrates in itself Larkin's particular kind of *compassionate* despair at the human condition; and while we can all feel this, nothing in life need be despondently written off.

The extraordinarily succinct appropriateness with which Larkin's mature diction works is evident in the opening:

> Slowly the women file to where he stands
> Upright in rimless glasses, silver hair,
> Dark suit, white collar. Stewards tirelessly
> Persuade them onwards to his voice and hands,
> Within whose warm spring rain of loving care
> Each dwells some twenty seconds.

The words enact exactly the appearance and posture of the healer, ministering to the ceaseless throng of women who pass for 'some twenty seconds' through his hands, telling him 'What's wrong'. Any harsher note of irony than the 'twenty seconds' and the 'warm spring rain' (infinitely gentle in its reproach) would mar the quality of sympathy and tip the poem over into anger or cynicism. The women move on in silence, weeping, reacting to the unfamiliar touch of kindness:

Moustached in flowered frocks they shake:
By now, all's wrong. In everyone there sleeps
A sense of life lived according to love.
To some it means the difference they could make
By loving others, but across most it sweeps
As all they might have done had they been loved.
That nothing cures.

'Faith Healing' is plainly not about just one healing service, but generally, and movingly, about the whole role—the deep and terrible necessity—of love in life.

'All they might have done had they been loved.' Larkin is careful never to suggest that happiness may be somehow arranged if only the proper steps could be taken. In 'Love Songs in Age' a widow is looking at the sheet music she has kept since she was young (conjured, in visual terms, with immense skill):

Relearning how each frank submissive chord
        Had ushered in
Word after sprawling hyphenated word,
And the unfailing sense of being young
Spread out like a spring-woken tree

But love had never solved, or satisfied, or set anything in her life 'unchangeably in order', and the time for hoping that it might is now gone. Already, the young marrieds, in 'Afternoons', sense something 'pushing them/To the side of their own lives'. The possibility of happiness in Larkin's poems about love finally seems something very meagre and elusive indeed.

Several poems in *The Whitsun Weddings* resume the fundamental Larkin themes of choice and purpose in life from where he left off in *The Less Deceived*; saying it all again with increasing power. One of them, 'Toads Revisited', is a sequel to 'Toads' in the earlier book, and written in similar quatrains. But the non-working alternative to the life of sober routine (that, at least, supports him on his way 'down Cemetery Road') is now more scaring and less enterprising. It consists of

Being one of the men
You meet of an afternoon:
Palsied old step-takers,
Hare-eyed clerks with the jitters,

Waxed-fleshed out-patients
Still vague from accidents,
And characters in long coats
Deep in the litter-baskets

Yet the life of tidy habits was one that 'Mr Bleaney' relished. Bleaney, former inhabitant of the wretched lodgings resignedly taken by the speaker in the poem of that title ('Bed, upright chair, sixty-watt bulb, no hook/Behind the door, no room for books or bags') represents a form of mediocre living from which the poet is theoretically emancipated. Yet, in renting the dreadful room, the latter has found himself in Mr Bleaney's position; it's no great consolation to *realize* this, either.

In 'Self's the Man', Larkin offers one of his comic, cruel depictions of the 'happy' family life he has gladly escaped. Arnold chose to marry, so nowadays

when he finishes supper
Planning to have a read at the evening paper
It's *Put a screw in this wall*—
He has no time at all,

With the nippers to wheel round the houses
And the hall to paint in his old trousers
And that letter to her mother
Saying *Won't you come for the summer.*

But Arnold's choice of marriage was deliberate, and the only difference between him and the poet is that the latter was more adept at avoiding what might drive him crazy. Or—and the hesitation carries a world of doubt and fear about his single existence—he *supposes* he was. This is Larkin amusingly yet scaringly pointing up the dilemmas again, pausing unnervingly at those moments of profound self-doubt (or more simply, sheer panic) which occasionally overtake most men—and exploring the terror. But if we are to believe one of his very best poems, 'Dockery and Son', there is really no question of choice or freedom at all: we are all predestined to, controlled by, the kind of life we happen to be leading.

Against the refined pessimism of these poems any offer of something positive seems an inadequate counterbalance. And yet paradoxically, in his fourth and best book, *High Windows*, published in 1974, alongside poems of the most intense gloom and alarm, Larkin develops the affirmative features of his talent. The exquisiteness of creative solitude is sharpened; the value of certain sorts of ritual observance is more strongly stressed; and the sense of hope to be found *somewhere*, happiness to be available for *some* people, is increased.

In *High Windows*, once again, some of the moments of utmost seriousness are approached through comedy, even broad comedy. In 'Posterity', Larkin sees the far future as holding nothing better than Jake Balokowsky, an American research student bored with having to write his biography. Larkin is tedious to Jake because his problems and anxieties were not attributable to any colourful aberrations. The poet was merely

> One of those old-type *natural* fouled-up guys.

The poem is an oblique onslaught on sensation-seeking in the modern world; and, implicitly, a defence of a passing world in which it was possible and comprehensible to be 'fouled-up' in the private self without recourse to, say, drugs or other external stimuli. And 'Vers de Société' approaches the topic of solitariness and privacy versus sociability through a dilemma over a party invitation. Initially, in the poet's mind, the invitation (in italics) is awarded a brusque reply:

> *My wife and I have asked a crowd of craps*
> *To come and waste their time and ours: perhaps*
> *You'd care to join us?* In a pig's arse, friend.

Nothing would be worse than the misery of party small-talk, and he resents the way in which it has been instilled that '*All solitude is selfish*' and '*Virtue is social*'; (in 'Sympathy in White Major' the hollow sociability of the selfless 'good chap' is held up to ridicule). But he sees how being sociable could represent something intrinsically decent: an effort to behave well towards others. The trouble is that he has uneasy personal reasons for finally accepting the invitation: a genuine dread of loneliness, a feeling that solitude is most enjoyed in youth, and that 'The time is shorter now for company'.

But the themes of how to live, of loneliness, age and death are also treated in *High Windows*, pregnantly and alarmingly, in poems which have no trace of humour at all. Larkin increasingly feels he can face these subjects directly in his most ambitious poems, without the hesitation, the slightly apologetic flavour, which humour suggests. In the three major poems of the collection, 'Livings', 'The Old Fools' and 'The Building', absolute solemnity (in the last two, a terrible, appalled solemnity) is maintained from the beginning in the development of the central ideas. All three are worth a close look.

'Livings' is one of Larkin's most impressive and startling poems: three separate ways of living, in different circumstances and different periods, are placed together and contemplated as samples of imaginable human existence. For each, the poet chooses a character. In the first section it is a travelling dealer in agricultural goods, in the 1920s; in the third it is a don among his fellow-clerks in late seventeenth-century Oxford. In the second, an astonishing centre-piece, Larkin is nearest to showing his own existence. The speaker is a lighthouse-keeper, alone in the midst of 'the salt/Unsown stirring fields' of water, the nearest human beings as remote as the 'lit shelved liners' which 'Grope like mad worlds westward'. Few of his poems illustrate so finely the full range of Larkin's talent and the richness of his subject-matter. The trappings of the hotel in I are done with entrancing authenticity, though it is 1929 and it will not last long. The invocation of the larger, colder world outside the secure scholars' den in III suggests the vulnerability of *that* living. And between them rears up the poet's precarious vantage-point, which is paradoxically more secure: the lighthouse symbolizing both creativity and intense loneliness. No kind of life, or living in the sense of a job, is safe; but awareness of the situation *is* a kind of mysterious advantage.

'The Old Fools' could lay claim to being Larkin's most desolating poem to date, a literal account of senility as accurate in its perceptions as 'Faith Healing', yet far more chilling and comfortless. It begins by looking disgustedly (but still not harshly) at the mere hopeless *un*awareness of the very old:

> What do they think has happened, the old fools,
> To make them like this? Do they somehow suppose
> It's more grown-up when your mouth hangs open
> and drools,
> And you keep on pissing yourself, and can't remember
> Who called this morning?

Age could well be a condition in which one imagines it is still possible to put back the clock, but how can the old ignore that approaching oblivion which is not (unlike that of the womb) a preliminary to birth.

> a unique endeavour
> To bring to bloom the million-petalled flower
> Of being here

(This magnificent image temporarily counters the repellent realism of the opening lines.) Or it may be that senility is a baffled mental alternation between vague pleasures of the past and the starkness of a present lived 'below/Extinction's alp'. Whatever it is, we shall all discover the truth in time. The poem is horrifyingly, levelly truthful and, this time, scarcely compassionate because that cannot be the point. What Larkin achieves in 'The Old Fools' is an appraisal of extreme old age which makes most other attempts to represent it seem false and unsuitable, whether done through sentimentality, or contrived realism, or black comedy.

It is, however, 'The Building' which qualifies as Larkin's finest poem of all in *High Windows*, and this is a masterpiece by any standards. Put simply, 'The Building' is about a clean new hospital, its out-patient waiting-rooms, its wards and corridors, the view of the outside from its windows. On this level it is a feat of harrowingly specific observation. But one cannot read the poem even once without knowing that much more than this is going on in it. 'The Building' is about the whole state of human living seen as a hospital. The people in its waiting-rooms are

> Humans, caught
> On ground curiously neutral, homes and names
> Suddenly in abeyance: some are young,
> Some old, but most at that vague age that claims
> The end of choice, the last of hope

Being in this building (being alive at all?) signifies the end of the false dreams the world offered, the start of the true sense of death. On a more literal, less allegorical, level, the hospital must somehow fulfil the role the Church has lost and *oppose* the sense of death:

> That is what it means,
> This clean-sliced cliff; a struggle to transcend
> The thought of dying, for unless its powers
> Outbuild cathedrals nothing contravenes
> The coming dark

But the 'unless' is important; it is by no means certain that the building can, in its secular role, do any better than the cathedrals in their lost, religious one.

Even if the articulation of pure despair has become more refined and bleak in *High Windows*, the interest in the value and significance of rituals and observances faithfully maintained has become more intent. This is something which Larkin increasingly uses as a method of affirming; a more indirect way of holding back 'the coming dark'. Thus, in 'To the Sea' he is delighted and reassured to find remembered seaside customs of his childhood still enacted on the crowded beaches. If 'Toads Revisited' paid grudging respect to work habits, 'To the Sea' finds a more positive virtue in habits of play:

> If the worst
> Of flawless weather is our falling short,
> It may be that through habit these do best,

Coming to water clumsily undressed
Yearly; teaching their children by a sort
Of clowning; helping the old, too, as they ought.

'Show Saturday' works towards a related kind of conclusion through a wonderful accumulation of concrete detail, the poet moving through the enclosures, the stalls and the tents of the seething field, watching the people drift home, concluding that the Show is good and valuable because it is

> something people do,
> Not noticing how time's rolling smithy-smoke
> Shadows much greater gestures; something they share
> That breaks ancestrally each year into
> Regenerate union. Let it always be there.

The regularity, the 'ancestral' quality of these activities is significant. Larkin's lack of hope or expectations for individual men is partly compensated for by the strength inherent in some communal rituals, performed regularly in the same places and perpetuated by the will of men in general (they can even be funeral customs, in 'Dublinesque'). Working against all this, of course, is the mindless destruction of rural England deplored in 'Going, Going' and the substitution of the worship of money for the duties of an imperial role in 'Homage to a Government' (where Larkin's conservatism, to the distaste of some readers, begins to take on a large 'C').

And there is at least one other pair of balancing opposites in *High Windows*. On the one hand, Larkin is still unable to think that there may be any kind of sure path to felicity in life. In 'This Be The Verse' he adopts a cynical *persona* for a poem which takes parenthood to be undesirable since, through it, 'Man hands on misery to man'. In 'Annus Mirabilis' he celebrates the release of others from sexual restraint (probably after the arrival of the contraceptive pill) with manifest irony: the implication is that happiness does not really lie in *that*. In the memorable title-poem, the current freedom of the young from fear in sex is compared with the new freedom from religious forebodings in his own youth; but both freedoms seem unimportant beside the

contemplation of some serene, indefinable purity represented
by (at the end of the poem)

> the thought of high windows:
> The sun-comprehending glass,
> And beyond it, the deep blue air, that shows
> Nothing, and is nowhere, and is endless.

Beyond the deep blue air itself might lie death; or life. The
question stays unresolved.

Such poems all, in varying degrees, take a pessimistic view
of human existence. Opposed to these thoughts, however, is
the recurrent reflection that others, particularly the young,
might still find happiness in expectation. For all its traps and
disappointments this is still a world in which (in 'The Trees',
the latest of several Larkin spring poems) branches can seem
to say 'Begin afresh, afresh, afresh'. Looking at the moon (as
so often) in 'Sad Steps' he rejects pretentious, literary thoughts
and sees how

> the plain
> Far-reaching singleness of that wide stare
>
> Is a reminder of the strength and pain
> Of being young; that it can't come again,
> But is for others undiminished somewhere.

And with 'How Distant', while the experience of youth is
now remote from him, as the title suggests, he can nevertheless affirm its powerful sense of hopefulness:

> This is being young,
> Assumption of the startled century
>
> Like new store clothes,
> The huge decisions printed out by feet
> Inventing where they tread,
> The random windows conjuring a street.

In one obvious sense *High Windows* is Larkin's finest
collection because there are simply more excellent poems in
it than in any previous volume. But another reason for such a

judgement would lie in the way in which all the various Larkin themes and motifs have here been brought together in a beautifully and precisely adjusted balance, and shown to us in an ever more confident and resonant use both of verse forms and of that immensely varied and flexible language that he has made his own.

Larkin's early association, in the mid-1950s, with the loose grouping of poets known as 'the Movement'—Kingsley Amis, Robert Conquest, Donald Davie, D. J. Enright, Thom Gunn, John Holloway, Elizabeth Jennings, John Wain—placed him among writers who were almost unanimously concerned to have their poetry lucid, tidy and technically smooth. In this company, his own distinctive technical skills, the special subtlety in his adaptation of a very personal colloquial mode to the demands of tight forms, were not immediately seen to be outstanding; but his strengths as a craftsman have increasingly come to be regarded as one of the hallmarks of his talent. Although one first observes the argument of the poetry, and the way in which imagery mostly derived from everyday living is ordered so as to express the deepest, sometimes the most alarming, feeling, close attention to Larkin's technical means show how much a care for perfection within his chosen forms contributes to the total effect.

As early as the first poems in *The Less Deceived*, Larkin's technical ease and command is evident. 'Lines on a Young Lady's Photograph Album' depends, for its half-humorous, half-serious, tone, on the skilful handling of a flexible decasyllabic line and precise rhyming. 'Wedding Wind' uses longer lines of varying length for a more meditated lyrical effect, introducing a pattern of less regular rhymes which unobtrusively tighten and control the structure of the poem. In other places in the book, he uses free verse (for example, in a lyric like 'Coming' and a disarming fantasy like 'If, My Darling'), though free verse is rare in his work and is used in a restrained way. And in the ingenious structuring of poems like 'No Road' and 'Wires' (with its adroit 'palindrome' of rhymes over the eight lines: abcd dcba) he displays an inventiveness with form that is somewhat reminiscent of his admired Hardy. But it is in the elaborate stanza of 'Church

Going' that the full sweep and range of Larkin's technical resourcefulness first becomes apparent.

The impressive, nine-line rhyming verses of 'Church Going', enabling a powerful and moving argument to develop through an extended treatment of the theme which mounts in grandeur as the poem proceeds, point forward to the eight-, nine-, ten- and twelve-line stanzas of 'Here', 'Faith Healing', 'Dockery and Son' and the title-poem in *The Whitsun Weddings*, and to poems like 'To the Sea', 'The Old Fools' and 'Show Saturday' in *High Windows*; and are the vehicle of Larkin's major statements in poetry. Larkin has never written easily. He composes slowly, and feels lucky if he writes more than one or two poems in a year. One would guess that the achievement of the large structures of these poems is very difficult for him. But any sense of effort or contrivance is utterly absent: the diction of the poems, the beautifully judged selection of imagery, fit into frameworks which support and enhance them with immense metrical skill. The short, four-syllable second line in each stanza of 'The Whitsun Weddings' creates an emphatic pause of deliberation before the verse continues with its flood of detail, and its meditations upon the detail. A short final line to every verse of 'The Old Fools' provides a chilling question ('Why aren't they screaming?'), or a link with the succeeding verse, or—at the end—a coldly final climax.

Yet Larkin's shorter poems, less outwardly remarkable in technical terms, may be no less skilful in the means employed: rhythms, stanza-forms and line-lengths which enable him to achieve a comic or sardonic tone in 'Sunny Prestatyn' (where the comedy turns suddenly to menace) or 'Naturally the Foundation will Bear Your Expenses'; or a memorable lyricism in the cadences of 'Cut Grass' and 'Trees'; or a triumphant surprise in 'The Explosion'. 'The Explosion', which concludes *High Windows*, is written in a line which echoes Longfellow's *Hiawatha*, a rhythm which has been used by English poets almost exclusively for the purpose of parody. The subject is a mine accident; and at the point at which the disaster occurs, Larkin *breaks* the well-known, regular, marching rhythm with a masterly use of changed emphasis and of punctuation:

Down the lane came men in pitboots
Coughing oath-edged talk and pipe-smoke,
Shouldering off the freshened silence.

One chased after rabbits; lost them;
Came back with a nest of lark's eggs;
Showed them; lodged them in the grasses.

So they passed in beards and moleskins,
Fathers, brothers, nicknames, laughter,
Through the tall gates standing open.

At noon, there came a tremor; cows
Stopped chewing for a second; sun,
Scarfed as in a heat-haze, dimmed.

'The Explosion' is an extraordinary and compelling poem
in many ways; but not the least of its qualities lies in Larkin's
capacity to astonish by the magnificent judgement with
which he brings off, so movingly and unexpectedly, this
technical stroke.

IV

Apart from his poetry, Philip Larkin has published two
novels, *Jill* and *A Girl in Winter*, both written in his early
twenties; and has assembled in *All What Jazz* seven years of
the jazz reviews he has contributed to the *Daily Telegraph*. He
edited the new *Oxford Book of Twentieth-Century English
Verse* (a volume which succeeded the one compiled by
W. B. Yeats in 1936). And there is a small body of poetry
review articles, so far uncollected, which casts interesting
light on Larkin's preferences in poetry, especially the poetry
of his own time.

The two novels date from the period immediately after
The North Ship; and eight years elapse between the second of
them and the publication of *The Less Deceived*. Although
neither book is outstanding, they are both better than their
author assumes them to be; and might have seemed, set
alongside the first volume of poems, to point to a future for
Larkin as an able and sensitive novelist rather than a major
poet.

Jill (1946) is about the first, and disastrous, term spent by a working-class boy, John Kemp, at Oxford. The year is 1940, and the undergraduate life Larkin describes wavers between carrying on as if the Second World War did not exist and accepting that unpalatable fact. Oxford is thoroughly settled into the wartime atmosphere: food is getting scarcer, 'blackouts' cover the windows, square brick air-raid shelters stand in the streets, alarming news arrives of devastating bombing attacks on distant cities. The author's principal concern, however, is with the personal fortunes of the humble John Kemp. John is the grammar school son of an ex-policeman, and has been selected and crammed for his scholarship by a coldly efficient English master (a remarkable study in dedicated, calculating mediocrity).

Arriving at his Oxford college, John finds he has to share rooms with Christopher Warner, a 'hearty' from a minor public school who has already gathered a small clique of rowdy companions. Their life is socially smarter and faster than John's; and the shy working-class boy, fascinated, is drawn incongruously and calamitously into it. Overhearing some wounding conversation about himself between Christopher and his girl friend Elizabeth, John responds to the impact of their expansive middle-class living by inventing an imaginary sister at a boarding school: the Jill of the title. Jill is someone round whom he can weave a fantasy life to compete with the glamorous reality of Christopher, his friends and his mother. But fantasy transmutes itself into fact, with an actual Jill turning up in the form of a young cousin of Elizabeth's. John's idealization and pursuit of the real girl—his 'hallucination of innocence'—ends in disaster: a drunken attempt to kiss her, the pitiable humiliation of a ducking in a pool, the term seen out in the College sick bay.

Jill makes numerous points about the nastiness of the class system, the resorts of the lonely, and the hazards of fantasy living; and makes them in a perceptive and moving way. Larkin is indubitably talented, here, in most departments of the novelist's art. His narrative has pace and surprise, there is variety and depth in the characterization, his ear for dialogue is hardly less than perfect. He also introduces one especially attractive and startling invention: the affectionate pastiche of

27

a girls' school story which Larkin has John Kemp compose as part of his exploration of the imaginary Jill. Again, though the compass of the novel is narrow (neither the academic life of the university, nor the student life outside John's orbit, is given any development), *Jill* catches the feel of living in this period with more than credible accuracy. It is, in fact, one of the better novels written about England during the Second World War, not so much for any conscious documentary effort put into it as for Larkin's characteristic scrupulousness in getting all the background details right. But neither *Jill* nor its successor equal in achievement the best that was eventually to come in Larkin's mature verse; and there is not much in the second novel to suggest that his talent for fiction could have diversified in such remarkable ways as his talent for poetry.

A Girl in Winter (1947) again has a wartime setting, and again places the central character in a position of acute psychological isolation. But this time the author himself is inventing a girl character, and Katherine Lind is no fantasy, but a real young woman set in a depressingly real world of dingy, humiliating routines and unattractive colleagues. Katherine is a foreign girl who finds herself (the exact circumstances are left unclear) employed in a library in an English provincial city. Her life is a desperately lonely one. She does not feel she can really try to resume acquaintance with the well-to-do family who entertained her as their son's school pen-friend shortly before the war; yet she finally writes a letter making tentative contact with them when she fortuitously finds a reference to the daughter of the family in a newspaper.

This is the first third of the book. The middle third is an extended flashback to Katherine's pre-war English visit. There is more than a hint of fantasy and idealization in the treatment of the Fennels' home, and family life, and in the social ease and maturity of the sixteen-year-old Robin. Then, in the final section, the story returns to the present, and deals with the changed, grown-up Robin's arrival at Katherine's lodgings in response to her letter; a soldier wanting a bed, which she grants him with an implicit acceptance of the fact of the present as something closer and more relevant than any dream of the past.

A Girl in Winter is widely regarded as an advance on *Jill* in technique and in imaginative range. Certainly the creation of Katherine Lind is impressive, and the resolution of the novel is both more ambitious and more satisfying than the abruptly unpleasant termination of the earlier book. Yet something is lost in Larkin's slight shift from a world of concrete, experienced reality in the Oxford of *Jill* to the memories and speculations in the mind of Katherine, however convincing the drab wartime world from which she retreats into them. *A Girl in Winter* leaves a sense of things happening out of time, of actions performed by characters imagined rather than people seen and known. If the tangible Oxford setting of *Jill* anticipates the wide-ranging social observation which strengthens so many of the later poems, *A Girl in Winter* is in many respects suggestive of the atmosphere of *The North Ship*, with a similar vague seeking after lonely fulfilment and release: in this sense it takes a step back. The development of the full strength of the later poetry seems to follow more directly from the first novel, and we may not need to regret Larkin's failure, despite considerable effort, to complete a third work of fiction.

Larkin has contributed reviews of new jazz records and books to the *Daily Telegraph* since 1961, and *All What Jazz: A Record Diary, 1961–8* (published in 1970) brings together his monthly articles from that period. Larkin's jazz journalism is just occasionally rather stiff and didactic, but more often relaxed, readable and informative: the book is very valuable as a comprehensive chronicle of jazz activity in the 1960s. He is, as might be expected, conservative in his taste in jazz. The driving-force of his enthusiasm is nostalgia for the departed jazz world of his own youth which, he sadly acknowledges, has gradually yielded to the challenge of a new jazz which he cannot enjoy. The last paragraph of his Introduction to *All What Jazz* defines his situation. It is poignantly, and darkly, devoted to portraying his readers, and has the tone and detail of some Larkin poems:

My readers . . . Sometimes I imagine them, sullen fleshy inarticulate men, stockbrokers, sellers of goods, living in thirty-year-old detached houses among the golf courses of Outer London, husbands of ageing and bitter wives they first seduced to Artie

Shaw's 'Begin the Beguine' or The Squadronaires' 'The Nearness of You'; fathers of cold-eyed lascivious daughters on the pill, to whom Ramsay MacDonald is coeval with Rameses II, and cannabis-smoking jeans-and-bearded Stuart-haired sons whose oriental contempt for 'bread' is equalled only by their insatiable demand for it . . . men whose first coronary is coming like Christmas; who drift, loaded helplessly with commitments and obligations and necessary observances, into the darkening avenues of age and incapacity, deserted by everything that once made life sweet. These I have tried to remind of the excitement of jazz, and tell where it may still be found.

Earlier in this Introduction, Larkin has charted his early love of the old jazz, at school and Oxford, and the dismay with which he came to the experiments of Monk, Davis, Coltrane, The Jazz Messengers, above all Charlie Parker. He mentions how he tried, patiently, to like innovation in jazz, and failed, and for a time muted his distaste when it came to writing about the records. He could appreciate the social and musical reasons for change, but he rapidly began to suspect the vocabulary in which the new jazz was discussed:

. . . there was something about the books I was now reading that seemed oddly familiar. This *development*, this *progress*, this *new language* that was more *difficult*, more *complex* . . . Of course! This was the language of criticism of modern painting, modern poetry, modern music.

And the term 'modern', he goes on to say, when applied to art 'denotes a quality of irresponsibility peculiar to this century, known sometimes as modernism'. 'Modernism' in all its forms, and the critical journalism which goes with it, receives a comprehensive denunciation: Picasso, Pound and Parker, and for that matter, Henry Moore and James Joyce, are all dealing in

irresponsible exploitations of technique in contradiction of human life as we know it . . . [modernism] helps us neither to enjoy nor endure. It will divert us as long as we are prepared to be mystified or outraged, but maintains its hold only by being more mystifying or more outrageous: it has no lasting power.

In this sustained attack on the modern we have a key to Larkin's whole aesthetic. His views on jazz are closely paralleled by his personal judgements on modern poets. (In trying to mute and adapt those views, in order to be fair, and representative, in compiling his *Oxford Book of Twentieth-Century English Verse*, he arrives at a most uneasy compromise. The book has all those who surely *must* be included; but the addition of a large number of others who have written single poems, sometimes odd poems, which Larkin happens to like, overbalances and weakens the anthology. It conveys a most misleading impression of the character and quality of English poetry in our time.) Larkin's principal and, of course, fruitful admirations in poetry are for writers who have either pre-dated modernism or evaded it: Hardy, William Barnes, Wilfred Owen, Stevie Smith, John Betjeman. Thomas Hardy (a benign successor to Yeats as an influence on the young Larkin) receives the highest praise: Larkin has said that he would not be without one poem of the Hardy *Collected Poems*. And John Betjeman, often patronized by the sophisticated as a joke-figure for his love of the old and the once-unfashionable (the art and architecture of the Victorians), becomes something very different in Larkin's notice of the *Collected Poems* in 1959—

one of the rare figures on whom the aesthetic appetites of an age pivot and swing round to face an entirely new direction.

Betjeman is not only admired for writing poetry that is socially exact, that accepts the life of his times, that honestly faces up to death, that is characterized by robustness and 'vivacious precision'—descriptions which would mostly fit Larkin—but also praised because he rejects modernism, and also appeals to a wide public. One of the cardinal sins of modernism for Larkin is its ostensible separation of artist from audience, and in an earlier piece, a sort of extended preface to one of his rare reviews of new poetry, Larkin declares the need for poetry to try to move towards the reader:

at bottom poetry, like all art, is inextricably bound up with giving pleasure, and if a poet loses his pleasure-seeking audience he has lost the only audience worth having.

It is easy to imagine that Larkin sees his own poetry as deriving from, or at least consistent with, these points of view about the modern in art, and these admirations. It is indeed true that many of his readers find pleasure and interest in Larkin's poetry for its apparent accessibility and its cultivation of verse forms that seem reassuringly traditional rather than 'modernist' in respect of rhyme and metre. But what happens in the personal practice of a poet is often a very different thing from what a poet formulates in the way of attitudes towards other people's poetry and his own. There is much more in Larkin's poetry than the ready appeal of its surfaces; and for that matter, much more that is 'difficult' and 'complex'—and profound—than might be expected after his statements on modernism. In something of the manner in which a dedicatedly experimental artist may be closer to the tradition than he imagines, an artist who avows traditionalism may be making it newer than he believes.

Posterity, which, simply because Larkin has lived and written, may have rather more sense and sensitivity than he fears, will perhaps sort out the paradox: Larkin has looked for his values to the past and the customs deriving from it, seeing in the present only the irreversible recession of all innocence, worth and sweetness from human living, and in the future nothing more than a process of unbearable decline and death, to be faced and defined with unflinching precision. Yet he has made out of this bitter, unalterable situation a poetry that is indisputably modern in its content and its cadences, and is wrought excitingly out of the English of our own time; a poetry which catches and makes beautiful the stuff of the experience of common men in the twentieth century.

PHILIP LARKIN

A Select Bibliography

(Place of publication London, unless stated otherwise)

Separate Works:
THE NORTH SHIP (1945). *Poems*
—new edition, with an introduction by the author, 1966.
JILL (1946). *Novel*
—new edition, with an introduction by the author, 1964.
A GIRL IN WINTER (1947). *Novel*
—new edition, 1956.
XX POEMS; privately printed (1951).
FANTASY POETS, No. 21; Eynsham (1954). *Poems*
THE LESS DECEIVED; Hessle, Yorkshire (1955). *Poems*
—3rd ed., 1956.
THE WHITSUN WEDDINGS: Poems (1964).
ALL WHAT JAZZ: A Record diary, 1961–68 (1970). *Jazz criticism*
HIGH WINDOWS (1974). *Poems*

Works Edited by Philip Larkin:
NEW POEMS, 1958, edited by Philip Larkin, Louis MacNeice and Bonamy
   Dobrée (1958). *Anthology*
THE OXFORD BOOK OF TWENTIETH-CENTURY ENGLISH VERSE; Oxford
   (1973). *Anthology*

Gramophone Records:
PHILIP LARKIN READS *The Less Deceived*; Hessle, Yorkshire (1958).
PHILIP LARKIN READS AND COMMENTS ON *The Whitsun Weddings*;
   Hessle, Yorkshire (1965).
PHILIP LARKIN READS *High Windows* (1975).

Some Critical and Other Studies:
'Auden's (and Empson's) Heirs', by F. W. Bateson, *Essays in Criticism*
   (Oxford), January 1957.
'The Poetry of Philip Larkin: A Note on Transatlantic Culture', by
   A. R. Jones, *Western Humanities Review*, XVI, Spring 1962, 143–52.
RULE AND ENERGY: Trends in British Poetry Since the Second World
   War, by John Press (1963).
THE NEW UNIVERSITY WITS AND THE END OF MODERNISM, by William Van
   O'Connor; Carbondale (1963).

THE PELICAN GUIDE TO ENGLISH LITERATURE; Harmondsworth (1964)
—Vol. 7, *The Modern Age*, includes 'Poetry Today', by Charles Tomlinson.

'Down Cemetery Road', by D. J. Enright, *New Statesman*, 28 February 1964.

'*The Whitsun Weddings*', by Ian Hamilton, *London Magazine*, May 1964.

'Engagement, or Withdrawal? Some notes on the Poetry of Philip Larkin', by John Wain, *Critical Quarterly*, VI, Summer 1964, 167–78.

'Four Conversations: Philip Larkin', by Ian Hamilton, *London Magazine*, November 1964.

'*The Whitsun Weddings*', by Colin Falck, *The Review*, December 1964.

A VISION OF REALITY: A Study of Liberalism in Twentieth-Century Verse, by Frederick Grubb (1965).

'A True Poet', by Christopher Ricks, *New York Review of Books*, 28 January 1965, 10–11.

THE NEW POETRY: An Anthology selected and introduced by A. Alvarez; Harmondsworth (1966)
—discusses Larkin's poetry in the Introduction.

'The Wintry Drum: the Poetry of Philip Larkin', by P. Gardner, *Dalhousie Review*, XLVIII, Spring 1968, 88–99.

THE SURVIVAL OF POETRY: A Contemporary Survey, ed. Martin Dodsworth (1970)
—includes 'The Poetry of Philip Larkin', by Anthony Thwaite.

'Philip Larkin of England', by A. Kingsley Weatherhead, *Journal of English Literary History* (Johns Hopkins University), December 1971, 616–30.

PHILIP LARKIN, by David Timms; Edinburgh (1973)
—a book-length critical study.

POETRY TODAY, 1960–1973, by Anthony Thwaite; Harlow (1973)
—a British Council survey.

PHILIP LARKIN: Special issue of *Phoenix*; Stockport (1974)
—contains essays on Larkin by Frederick Grubb, George Hartley, Edna Longley, Christopher Ricks, Anthony Thwaite, David Timms and others.

'Wolves of Memory', by Clive James, *Encounter*, June 1974, 65–71.

'Philip Larkin: A Profile', by Dan Jacobson, *The New Review*, June 1974, 25–9.

'The Art of Debunkery', by Richard Murphy, *New York Review of Books*, 15 May 1975.

WRITERS AND THEIR WORK

HUME: Montgomery Belgion
SAMUEL JOHNSON: S. C. Roberts
POPE: Ian Jack
RICHARDSON: R. F. Brissenden
SHERIDAN: W. A. Darlington
CHRISTOPHER SMART: G. Grigson
SMOLLETT: Laurence Brander
STEELE, ADDISON: A. R. Humphreys
STERNE: D. W. Jefferson
SWIFT: J. Middleton Murry
SIR JOHN VANBRUGH: Bernard Harris
HORACE WALPOLE: Hugh Honour

Nineteenth Century:
MATTHEW ARNOLD: Kenneth Allott
JANE AUSTEN: S. Townsend Warner
BAGEHOT: N. St John-Stevas
THE BRONTËS: I & II: Winifred Gérin
BROWNING: John Bryson
E. B. BROWNING: Alethea Hayter
SAMUEL BUTLER: G. D. H. Cole
BYRON: I, II & III:
          Bernard Blackstone
CARLYLE: David Gascoyne
LEWIS CARROLL: Derek Hudson
COLERIDGE: Kathleen Raine
CREEVEY & GREVILLE: J. Richardson
DE QUINCEY: Hugh Sykes Davies
DICKENS: K. J. Fielding
    EARLY NOVELS: T. Blount
    LATER NOVELS: B. Hardy
DISRAELI: Paul Bloomfield
GEORGE ELIOT: Lettice Cooper
FERRIER & GALT: W. M. Parker
FITZGERALD: Joanna Richardson
ELIZABETH GASKELL: Miriam Allott
GISSING: A. C. Ward
THOMAS HARDY: R. A. Scott-James
          and C. Day Lewis
HAZLITT: J. B. Priestley
HOOD: Laurence Brander
G. M. HOPKINS: Geoffrey Grigson
T. H. HUXLEY: William Irvine
KEATS: Edmund Blunden
LAMB: Edmund Blunden
LANDOR: G. Rostrevor Hamilton
EDWARD LEAR: Joanna Richardson
MACAULAY: G. R. Potter

MEREDITH: Phyllis Bartlett
JOHN STUART MILL: M. Cranston
WILLIAM MORRIS: P. Henderson
NEWMAN: J. M. Cameron
PATER: Ian Fletcher
PEACOCK: J. I. M. Stewart
ROSSETTI: Oswald Doughty
CHRISTINA ROSSETTI: G. Battiscombe
RUSKIN: Peter Quennell
SIR WALTER SCOTT: Ian Jack
SHELLEY: G. M. Matthews
SOUTHEY: Geoffrey Carnall
LESLIE STEPHEN: Phyllis Grosskurth
R. L. STEVENSON: G. B. Stern
SWINBURNE: Ian Fletcher
TENNYSON: B. C. Southam
THACKERAY: Laurence Brander
FRANCIS THOMPSON: P. Butter
TROLLOPE: Hugh Sykes Davies
OSCAR WILDE: James Laver
WORDSWORTH: Helen Darbishire

Twentieth Century:
CHINUA ACHEBE: A. Ravenscroft
JOHN ARDEN: Glenda Leeming
W. H. AUDEN: Richard Hoggart
SAMUEL BECKETT: J-J. Mayoux
HILAIRE BELLOC: Renée Haynes
ARNOLD BENNETT: Kenneth Young
JOHN BETJEMAN: John Press
EDMUND BLUNDEN: Alec M. Hardie
ROBERT BRIDGES: J. Sparrow
ANTHONY BURGESS: Carol M. Dix
ROY CAMPBELL: David Wright
JOYCE CARY: Walter Allen
G. K. CHESTERTON: C. Hollis
WINSTON CHURCHILL: John Connell
R. G. COLLINGWOOD: E. W. F. Tomlin
I. COMPTON-BURNETT:
          R. Glynn Grylls
JOSEPH CONRAD: Oliver Warner
WALTER DE LA MARE: K. Hopkins
NORMAN DOUGLAS: Ian Greenlees
LAWRENCE DURRELL: G. S. Fraser
T. S. ELIOT: M. C. Bradbrook
T. S. ELIOT: The Making of
    'The Waste Land': M. C. Bradbrook